Handy Maine Genealogy Handbook

I0450614

By Gary L. Morris

©2015 Gary L. Morris

ISBN-13: 978-1507659700

ISBN-10: 1507659709

Table of Contents

Notes

Genealogical Research in Maine

Tracing your family history in Maine can be a fascinating trip through time. As part of the Massachusetts Commonwealth, Maine was among the original colonies, and as such there is a wealth of genealogical records to be found for the state. Tracking these records down can be an ominous task, as some may be in the archives and repositories of Massachusetts. Don't worry though, we know just where they are, and we'll show you which records you'll need, and help you to understand:

1. What they are
2. Where to find them
3. How to use them

These records can be found both online and off, so we'll introduce you to online websites, indexes and databases, as well as brick-and-mortar repositories and other institutions that will help with your research in Maine. So that you will have a more comprehensive understanding of these records, we have provided a brief history of the "Pine Tree State" to illustrate what type of records may have been generated during specific time periods. That information will assist you in pinpointing times and locations on which to focus the search for your Maine ancestors and their records.

A Brief History of Maine

Dozens of Native American tribes once inhabited Maine, including the warlike Micmacs and the more peaceful and numerous Abnakis. Two today only four tribes reside on reservations in Maine, the Penobscots, the Micmacs, the Maliseets, and the Passamaquoddies. It is thought the first Europeans to step ashore in Maine were a group of Vikings led by Leif Ericson who arrived 500 years before Christopher Columbus. The first settlement by Europeans was established at Popham in 1607 and Jamestown the same year. As the colony at Popham did not survive the harsh winter, Jamestown is considered as the first permanent settlement in America.

The 1920's saw many settlements established along the coast of Maine, though harsh conditions and attacks by Native Americans wiped out many of the early settlers. Only a half dozen settlements survived as Maine entered the 18th century, and by then Massachusetts had purchased the majority of the land that made up the area that is now the state of Maine. That arrangement lasted right up until Maine gained statehood in 1820.

Dispute over the ownership of Maine between England and France continued during the first half of the 18th century. The French supported the Native American raids on English settlers which led to the beginning of the French and Indian Wars in 1754. The war ended in 1763 with the Treaty of Paris which put an end to any French claims to the area.

After the Indian threat lessened the population of Maine began to grow, fueled by the offer from Massachusetts of one hundred acre lots for free to anyone who would settle in the Northern Province. By the end of the century, the population of Maine had risen from around 24,000 in 1763 to over 150,000. A raging mob seized tax documents in Falmouth in 1765, and custom agents were attacked frequently thereafter. Inspired by the Boston Tea Party in 1773, the residents of Maine staged their own version of the incident by burning a shipment of tea that was being stored at York. More than one thousand men from Maine were died during the Revolutionary War, trade was damaged extensively, and the principal city of Falmouth (now Portland) was utterly destroyed.

After the Revolutionary War resentment grew among the frontier settlers towards Massachusetts rule. When Massachusetts failed to protect the Maine settlers during the War of 1812, Maine pushed towards statehood, which was awarded in 1820. A state constitution was drafted, Portland elected as the capital, though in 1832 Augusta, a more centrally located city was elected the state capital.

Important Dates in Maine History

1604 - French contingency led by Pierre du Guast Sieur de Monts establishes first recorded European colony in Maine at the mouth of the St. Croix River.

1607 - British establish the Fort Popham Colony

1622 - Sir Ferdinando Gorges and John Mason are granted rights to lands which make up what is now Maine and New Hampshire. Gorges became the first person to title the territory "Maine."

1652 - Maine annexed by Massachusetts.

1675 - King Phillip's War begins between the English and the French and Indians for control of the North American territories.

1675 - 1763 - Conflict between the North American powers continues and eventually ends with France surrendering their holdings in the new world to the English.

1775 - First naval battle of the Revolutionary War occurs off the coast of Machias.

1775 - Benedict Arnold marches a band of revolutionaries through Maine in a failed attempt to capture British strongholds in Quebec City and Montreal.

1820 – Statehood

1842 - Border with Canada permanently settled

Famous Battles Fought in Maine

The **Battle of Portland Harbor** was the only Civil War that took place in Maine, and that was a naval battle that took place off the coast of modern day Portland. Over 80,000 men from however Maine fought for the Union side in the Civil War. Likewise there were no Revolutionary War land battles fought there, but three was a naval battle fought known as the **Burning of Falmouth**. The **Battle at Moore's Brook** was fought in Maine during King Philip's War

These battle accounts that do exist can be very effective in uncovering the military records of your ancestor. They can tell you what regiments fought in which battles, and often include the names and ranks of many officers and enlisted men.

Battle of Portland Harbor:
https://www.mpbn.net/News/MPBNNews/tabid/1159/ctl/ViewItem/mid/3762/ItemId/28762/Default.aspx

Burning of Falmouth, 1775:
http://www.revolutionarywar101.com/battles/751018-falmouth.html

Battle at Moore's Brook:
http://www.hampton.lib.nh.us/hampton/history/military/mooresbrook.htm

Common Maine Genealogical Issues and Resources to Overcome Them

Boundary Changes: Boundary changes are a common obstacle when researching Maine ancestors. You could be searching for an ancestor's record in one county when in fact it is stored in a different one due to historical county boundary changes. Some of those counties may even now be in Massachusetts or other states.

The **Atlas of Historical County Boundaries** can help you to overcome that problem. It provides a chronological listing of every boundary change that has occurred in the history of Maine.

Atlas of Historical County Boundaries link to: http://publications.newberry.org/ahcbp/documents/ME_Consolidated_Chronology.htm#Consolidated_Chronology

Name Changes: Surname changes, variations, and misspellings can complicate genealogical research. It is important to check all spelling variations. Soundex, a program that indexes names by sound, is a useful first step, but you can't rely on it completely as some name variations result in different Soundex codes. The surnames could be different, but the first name may be different too. You can also find records filed under initials, middle names, and nicknames as well, so you will need to **get creative with surname variations** and spellings in order to cover all the possibilities. For help with surname variations read our instructional article on **How to Use Soundex**.

get creative with surname variations: http://obituarieshelp.org/blog/?p=634

How to Use Soundex: http://obituarieshelp.org/blog/?p=505

Maine Genealogical Organizations and Archives

Genealogical resources include not only records, but the organizations that house them, or can direct you to them. These institutions include: *Archives, Libraries, Genealogical Societies, Family History Centers, Universities, Churches, and Museums.*

Following are links to their websites, their physical addresses, and a summary of the records you can find there.

Archives and Libraries

Maine State Archives - collection of genealogies, town histories, published vital records for towns in Maine and much of New England, materials on the Maritime Provinces of Canada, Civil War databases, city directories,

230 State Street
Augusta, Maine 04333
Tel: 207-287-5795

Mailing Address:
84 State House Station
Augusta, Maine 04333

Maine State Archives: http://www.maine.gov/sos/arc/

National Archives Northeast Region (Boston) – miscellaneous genealogical records such as ship's passenger lists, cemetery records, land records and military records pertaining to the Northeast Region which includes Connecticut, Maine, Massachusetts, New Hampshire, Rhode Island, and Vermont.

380 Trapelo Road
Waltham, MA 02154
Telephone: 617-647-8100
Fax: 617-647-8460

National Archives Northeast Region (Boston):
http://www.archives.gov/boston/

Bangor Public Library - Bangor Daily News Index, county histories, family histories published resources, city directories, military histories, Passenger/Immigrant Ship Information, State and Federal Census State Resources such as the Maine Register Town Histories

145 Harlow Street
Bangor, ME 04401
Telephone: 207-947-8336
Fax 207-945-6694

Bangor Public Library:
http://www.bpl.lib.me.us/LocalHistory/index_specialcollections.htm
l

Maine Genealogical and Historical Societies

Genealogical and historical societies have access to extensive catalogues of genealogical data. They are also able to offer expert guidance for genealogical researchers. Many members are professional genealogists who are most willing to share their expertise in finding ancestors.

Maine Historical Society – published and compiled genealogies, town histories, vital records, census records, city directories, town reports, maps, photographs, manuscripts, journals, and many other resources

489 Congress St.
Portland, ME 04101
Tel: 207-774-1822

Maine Historical Society: http://www.mainehistory.org/

Maine Franco-American Genealogy Society - documentation of marriages in New England and Canada, census records dating back to 1607, a vast collection of obituaries cut from newspapers, periodicals, database containing the birth and death records of all the church parishes in Beauce County Quebec from 1738-1900

Maine Franco-American Genealogy:
http://www.simplesite.com/MFGSWebsite/

Maine Jewry – Online site containing hundreds of years worth of oral histories, census extracts, burial records, and surname database containing 32,329 individual Jews with strong ties to Maine

Maine Jewry: http://www.mainejews.org/

Maine Mailing Lists

Mailing lists are internet based facilities that use email to distribute a single message to all who subscribe to it. When information on a particular surname, new records, or any other important genealogy information related to the mailing list topic becomes available, the subscribers are alerted to it. Joining a mailing list is an excellent way to stay up to date on Maine genealogy research topics. Rootsweb have an extensive listing of **Maine Mailing Lists** on a variety of topics.

Maine Mailing Lists link to:
http://lists.rootsweb.ancestry.com/index/usa/ME/misc.html

Maine Message Boards

A message board is another internet based facility where people can post questions about a specific genealogy topic and have it answered by other genealogists. If you have questions about a surname, record type, or research topic, you can post your question and other researchers and genealogists will help you with the answer. Be sure to check back regularly, as the answers are not emailed to you. The Maine message boards at **Rootsweb** are completely free to use.

Rootsweb:
http://boards.rootsweb.com/localities.northam.usa.states/mb.ashx

Maine Newspapers and Periodicals

Many genealogy periodicals and historical newspapers contain reprinted copies of family genealogies, transcripts of family Bible records, information about local records and archives, census indexes, church records, queries, land records, obituaries, court records, cemetery records, and wills. The following sites have historical Maine newspapers and periodicals that you can search online or on-site.

Bangor Public Library - **Bangor Daily News Index** – large database of Bangor newspapers dating from the early nineteenth century

145 Harlow Street
Bangor, ME 04401
Telephone: 207-947-8336
Fax 207-945-6694

Bangor Daily News Index:
http://www.bpl.lib.me.us/Periodicals/newspaper_holdings.html

Maine Historical Society – strong collection of historical nineteenth century Maine newspapers

489 Congress St.
Portland, ME 04101
Tel: 207-774-1822

Maine Historical Society:
http://www.mainehistory.org/library_overview.shtml#newspapers

Bates College Library – nationwide historical newspapers published between 1690 and 1922, Lewiston newspapers, 1861 to present

Bates College
2 Andrews Road
Lewiston, ME 04240
Phone: 207-786-6255

Bates College Library:
https://kent.bates.edu/erm/index.php/erm/find/type/News%20and%20Newspaper%20Archives%3A%20Maine

GenealogyBank.com – free searchable database of Maine newspaper archives, 1785–1950

GenealogyBank.com:
http://www.genealogybank.com/gbnk/newspapers/explore/USA/Maine/

Library of Congress Digital Newspaper Directory – free searchable database of historical U.S. newspapers dating from 1690-present

Library of Congress Digital Newspaper Directory:
http://chroniclingamerica.loc.gov/search/titles/

The Online Books Page – links to historical books and periodicals available for viewing online, dating from mid-16th century

The Online Books Page:
http://onlinebooks.library.upenn.edu/webbin/book//browse?type=lcsubc&key=Maine%20--%20History%20--%20Periodicals

NewspaperArchive.com – largest online database of historical newspapers in the world.

NewspaperArchive.com: http://newspaperarchive.com/

<u>Historical Maine Maps and Gazetteers</u>

Maps are an integral part of genealogical research. They help us to locate landmarks, towns, cities, parishes, states, provinces, waterways and roads and streets. They also help us to determine when and where boundary changes might have taken place, and give us a visualization of the area we're researching in.

For locating place names, a gazetteer is the best possible resource for any genealogist. Gazetteers are also sometimes called "place name dictionaries", and can help you to locate the area in which you need to conduct research. Below are links to the maps and gazetteers for research in Maine.

Peabody GNIS Service – Maine: http://peabody.research.yale.edu/cgi-bin/Query.GNIS?ST=Maine&SU=1

Color Landform Atlas – Maine: http://fermi.jhuapl.edu/states/me_0.html

1985 U.S. Atlas: http://www.livgenmi.com/1895/ME/

Maine Hometown Locator: http://maine.hometownlocator.com/

Maine City Directories

City directories are similar to telephone directories in that they list the residents of a particular area. The difference though is what is important to genealogists, and that is they pre-date telephone directories. You can find an ancestor's information such as their street address, place of employment, occupation, or the name of their spouse. A one-stop-shop for finding city directories in Maine is the **Maine Online Historical Directories** which contains a listing of every available online historical directory related to Maine.

Maine Online Historical Directories:
https://sites.google.com/site/onlinedirectorysite/Home/usa/me

Maine Historical Society – large collection of city directories for most of Maine which includes: Augusta, Bangor, Bath, Biddeford/Saco, Brunswick, Lewiston/Auburn, Portland 1824 to present, Rockland, Sanford, Westbrook/Gorham/Windham, Various Mitchell directories for many other smaller Maine towns, 1905 to 1907, plus the New England Business Directory and Gazetteer, 1900-1924, Maine Register, 1820 to present and Various County directories, late 1880s–1900

489 Congress St.
Portland, ME 04101
Tel: 207-774-1822

Maine Historical Society:
http://www.mainehistory.org/library_holdings.shtml#directories

Maine Genealogical Records

<u>Birth, Death, Marriage and Divorce Records</u> – Also known as vital records, birth, death, and marriage certificates are the most basic, yet most important records attached to your ancestor. The reason for their importance is that they not only place your ancestor in a specific place at a definite time, but potentially connect the individual to other relatives. Below is a list of repositories and websites where you can find Maine vital records.

Certified copies of birth, death, or marriage records from 1923 to the present are available from the **Office of Vital Records** or from the city or town where the event took place. Divorce records from 1892 through the present may also be obtained from the Office of Vital Records.

244 Water Street
Augusta, Maine 04330
Tel: 207-287-3181

Office of Vital Records link to:
http://www.maine.gov/dhhs/mecdc/public-health-systems/data-research/vital-records/order/index.shtml

Birth, death, and marriage records from 1892-1922 are available in the **Maine State Archives** research room or can be ordered by mail from the Archives from the following address:

Maine State Archives
State House Station 84
Augusta, ME 04333

Maine State Archives link to:
http://www.maine.gov/sos/arc/research/vitalrec.html

On Microfilm

Microfilm copies of birth, marriage, and death records from 1922-1955 are available for viewing in the State Archives research room. The State Archives also has the following indexes online that can be searched for free.

Searchable Marriage Indexo:
https://portal.maine.gov/marriage/archdev.marriage_archive.search_form

Searchable Death Index:
https://portal.maine.gov/death/archdev.death_archive.search_form

Family Search has the following indexes that can be searched for free online:

Maine Births and Christenings, 1739-1900:
https://familysearch.org/search/collection/1674856

Maine Deaths and Burials, 1841-1910:
https://familysearch.org/search/collection/1674914

Maine Marriages, 1771-1907:
https://familysearch.org/search/collection/1674915

Census Reports

Census records are among the most important genealogical documents for placing your ancestor in a particular place at a specific time. Like BDM records, they can also lead you to other ancestors, particularly those who were living under the authority of the head of household.

Federal census records for Maine exist from 1790–1930

Maine Historical Society – 1790–1930 entire state, AIS index books for Maine 1790–1850, 1860 York County index, 1850 Aroostook County and Mortality schedule, 1850 Census transcription of Maine towns, Black Census of Maine, 1800–1910

489 Congress St.
Portland, ME 04101
Tel: 207-774-1822

Maine Historical Society:
http://www.mainehistory.org/library_holdings.shtml#census

The **Free Census Project** has transcribed many Maine indexes and new material is added daily

Free Census Project: http://usgwcensus.org/cenfiles/me.htm

Access Genealogy – Maine county census records from 1790

Access Genealogy: http://www.accessgenealogy.com/census/Maine-census-records.htm

African American Census Schedules Online – slave schedules, mortality schedules, slave-owners census

African American Census Schedules Online:
http://www.afrigeneas.com/aacensus/ga/

Native Americans in Census Records (US National Archives)

Native Americans in Census Records:
http://www.archives.gov/research/census/native-americans/

Maine Church Records

Church and synagogue records are a valuable resource, especially for baptisms, marriages, and burials that took place before 1900. You will need to at least have an idea of your ancestor's religious denomination, and in most cases you will have to visit a brick and mortar establishment to view them.

Most church records are kept by the individual church, although in some denominations, records are placed in a regional archive or maintained at the diocesan level. Local Historical Societies are sometimes the repository for the state's older church records. Below are links archives that maintain church records, as well as a few databases that can be viewed online.

The **Family History Library** contains many church records from a variety of denominations on microfilm.

Family History Library:
http://familysearch.org/learn/wiki/en/Family_History_Library

Maine Historical Society - Many published and manuscript church records for Unitarian, Baptist, Quaker, Methodist, Congregational churches

489 Congress St.
Portland, ME 04101
Tel: 207-774-1822

Maine Historical Society:
http://www.mainehistory.org/library_holdings.shtml#church

Maine Franco-American Genealogy Society - documentation of marriages in New England and Canada, database containing the birth and death records of all the church parishes in Beauce County Quebec from 1738-1900

Maine Franco-American Genealogy Society:
http://www.simplesite.com/MFGSWebsite/

New England Historic Genealogical Society – wealth of material and resources for searching early Maine church records dating from 1642

99 - 101 Newbury Street
Boston, Massachusetts 02116, USA
Tel: 617-536-5740

New England Historic Genealogical Society:
http://www.americanancestors.org/genealogical-research-in-maines-oldest-county/

Central Repositories for Denominational Records

Most of the records of individual denominations are kept in central repositories. Below is a list of the major congregational archives for Maine with links to their websites, physical addresses, and contact information.

Baptist

American Baptist Historical Society
3001 Mercer University Dr.
Atlanta, Georgia 30341
Telephone: (678) 547-6680

American Baptist Historical Society: http://abhsarchives.org/

Church of Jesus Christ of Latter-day Saints (Mormons)

Early Mormon Church records for Maine can be found on film located at the LDS Family History Library in Salt Lake City and can be searched via the **Family History Library Catalog**

Family History Library Catalog:
https://familysearch.org/eng/Library/FHLC/frameset_fhlc.asp

Roman Catholic

Roman Catholic Diocese of Portland
P.O. Box 11559 (mailing address)
510 Ocean Avenue
Portland, Maine 04104-7559
Phone: (207) 773-6471

Roman Catholic Diocese of Portlando:
http://www.portlanddiocese.org/info.php?info_id=59

Congregational

The Congregational Library
14 Beacon Street
Boston, Massachusetts 02108
Phone: (617) 523-0470

The Congregational Library: http://www.14beacon.org/

Episcopal

Archives of the Diocese of Maine
Attn: Archivist
143 State Street
Portland, ME 04101
Phone: (207) 772-1953, ext. 137

Archives of the Diocese of Maine :
http://www.episcopalmaine.org/index.php?option=com_content&vie
w=article&id=116

<u>Methodist</u>

Boston University School of Theology Library
745 Commonwealth Avenue
Boston, MA 02215
Phone: (617) 353-1323

Boston University School of Theology Library:
http://www.bu.edu/sthlibrary/archives/

Maine Military Records

More than 40 million Americans have participated in some time of war service since America was colonized. The chance of finding your ancestor amongst those records is exceptionally high. Military records can even reveal individuals who never actually served, such as those who registered for the two World Wars but were never called to duty.

Below are a number of links to websites and archives that contain Maine military records.

Maine State Archives - War of 1812 - Maine Militia Rolls and Rolls of Maine men serving in the U.S. Regular Army, Annual Inspection Returns 1810-1817 , Orders and Schedules, Revolutionary War Land Grants and Pension Applications, 1835 and 1838, Records of General Orders and of Special Orders and the Official Correspondence of the Office of the Adjutant General

230 State Street
Augusta, Maine 04333
Tel: 207-287-5795

Mailing Address:
84 State House Station
Augusta, Maine 04333

Maine State Archives link to:
http://www.maine.gov/sos/arc/research/military.html

U.S. National Archives – WWI Draft registration cards, casualties lists, WWI and WWII service records, Korean War records, Vietnam War records, Civil War and Spanish-American War records, and casualties lists.

U.S. National Archives:
http://www.archives.gov/research/military/veterans/online.html

Maine Historical Society – Adjutant General's Report, Maine, 1861–1866, Massachusetts Soldiers and Sailors of the Revolutionary War, Roster of Maine in the World War 1917–1919, Connecticut Military Record 1775-1848, Record of Connecticut Men in the War of Rebellion 1861 to 1865, Adjutant General's Report, New Hampshire, 1865, 1866, 1868, Adjutant General's Report, Massachusetts, 1863, 1864, 1865, Massachusetts Soldiers, Sailors, and Marines in the Civil War, Massachusetts Soldiers and Sailors of the Revolutionary War, Maine Record of the Massachusetts Volunteers, 1861–1865

489 Congress St.
Portland, ME 04101
Tel: 207-774-1822

Maine Historical Society:
http://www.mainehistory.org/library_holdings.shtml#census

US Department of Veterans Affairs Nationwide Gravesite Locator – includes information on veterans and their family members buried in veterans and military cemeteries having a government grave marker.

US Department of Veterans Affairs Nationwide Gravesite Locator: http://gravelocator.cem.va.gov/

You may also find your ancestor's military records in the following databases:

United States Index to Indian Wars Pension Files, 1892-1926 – military pension records of soldiers who fought in the Indian Wars between 1817 and 1898

United States Index to Indian Wars Pension Files, 1892-1926: https://familysearch.org/search/collection/1979427

United States Registers of Enlistments in the U.S. Army, 1798-1914 - index of men who enlisted in the United States Army, 1798-1914.

United States Registers of Enlistments in the U.S. Army, 1798-1914: https://familysearch.org/search/collection/1880762

United States Mexican War Pension Index, 1887-1926 - index to Mexican War pension files for service between 1846 and 1848

United States Mexican War Pension Index, 1887-1926: https://familysearch.org/search/collection/1979390

Civil War Soldiers Service Records - Service records for both Union and Confederate soldiers indexed by soldier's name, rank, and unit.

Civil War Soldier Service Records: http://go.fold3.com/civilwar_records/

Maine Cemetery Records

As convenient as it is to search cemetery records online, keep in mind that there are a few disadvantages over visiting a cemetery in person. They are:

- Tombstone information is not always accurately transcribed
- The arrangement of the graves in a cemetery can be crucial as family members are often buried next to each other or in the same grave.
- This arrangement is not always preserved in the alphabetical indexes that are found online.

With that information in mind, the following websites have databases that can be searched online for Maine Cemetery records.

Maine Tombstone Transcription Project - death and burial records

Maine Tombstone Transcription Project:
http://www.usgwtombstones.org/maine/maine.html

African American Cemeteries Online – African American, slave, and Native American cemetery records

African American Cemeteries Online:
http://africanamericancemeteries.com/ar/

Access Genealogy – huge database of Maine cemetery record transcriptions

Access Genealogy:
http://www.accessgenealogy.com/cemetery/maine-cemetery-records.htm

Find a Grave – over 100 million grave records can be searched on this site. Search can be conducted by name, location, or cemetery name.

Find a Grave: http://www.findagrave.com/

Interment.net - A free online database containing approximately 4 million cemetery records from around the world.

Interment.net: http://www.interment.net/

Billion Graves – as the name implies, you can search a billion records including headstone photos, transcriptions, cemetery records, and grave locations.

Billion Graves: http://billiongraves.com/pages/search/index.php#cemetery

Maine Obituaries

Obituaries can reveal a wealth about our ancestor and other relatives. You can search our **Maine Newspaper Obituaries Listings** from hundreds of Maine newspapers online for free.

Maine Newspaper Obituaries Listings: http://obituarieshelp.org/maine_newspaper_obituaries.html

Maine Wills and Probate Records

The documents found in a probate packet may include a complete inventory of a person's estate, newspaper entries, witness testimony, a copy of a will, list of debtors and creditors, names of executors or trustees, names of heirs. They can not only tell you about the ancestor you're currently researching, but lead to other ancestors.

Probate records in Maine are under the jurisdiction of the register of probate or the clerk of the probate court in each county. Copies of the original records may be obtained by contacting the **Probate Clerk of the Court Office** in the county where the event occurred.

Probate Clerk of the Court Office:
http://www.courts.state.me.us/maine_courts/district/directory.shtml

Other valuable sources of Maine Probate and Wills records are:

Maine Historical Society – Maine Wills, 1640–1760, Maine Probate, 1687–1800, Maine Province and Court Records, York County Will Abstracts to 1858, Lincoln County Records 1760–1800), Penobscot County Rcords, 1816–1866

489 Congress St.
Portland, ME 04101
Tel: 207-774-1822

Maine Historical Society:
http://www.mainehistory.org/library_holdings.shtml#census

Family Search has the following indexes that can be searched online for free:

Maine Androscoggin County, Probate Estate Files, 1854-1918:
https://familysearch.org/search/collection/2037995

Maine Aroostook County Deed Books, 1865-1900:
https://familysearch.org/search/collection/1447693

Maine Aroostook County, Probate Records, 1837-2007:
https://familysearch.org/search/collection/1415491

Maine County Probate Records, 1760-1979:
https://familysearch.org/search/collection/2040534

Maine Kennebec County Probate Estates Files, 1779-1915:
https://familysearch.org/search/collection/2040534

Maine Knox County Cemetery Records, ca. 1800-2007:
https://familysearch.org/search/collection/1386085

Maine Knox County, Probate Estate Files, 1861-1915:
https://familysearch.org/search/collection/1931808

Maine, Oxford County, Probate Estate Files, 1805-1915:
https://familysearch.org/search/collection/2040540

Maine, Piscataquis County, Deed Books, 1838-1902:
https://familysearch.org/search/collection/1447336

Maine, Somerset County, Probate Estate Files, 1809-1915:
https://familysearch.org/search/collection/2094263

Maine, Washington County Courthouse Records, 1785-1950:
https://familysearch.org/search/collection/1930294

Maine, York County, Probate Estate Files, 1690-1917:
https://familysearch.org/search/collection/2094226

Maine Immigration and Naturalization Records

The naturalization process generated many types of records, including petitions, declarations of intention, and oaths of allegiance. These records can provide family historians with information such as a person's birth date and place of birth, immigration year, marital status, spouse information, occupation, witnesses' names and addresses, and more.

The **US National Archives** has a huge collection of Ship's Passenger lists for Maine and the surrounding east coast ports where immigrants would have arrived. Remember, Maine was a part of Massachusetts until statehood, so many who immigrated there would have arrived in ports like Boston.

US National Archives link to:
http://www.archives.gov/research/immigration/passenger-arrival.html

The National Archives at Boston – Chinese immigration records

The National Archives at Boston
380 Trapelo Road
Waltham, Massachusetts
02452-6399

The National Archives at Boston:
http://www.archives.gov/boston/public/microfilm.html

Maine Historical Society – Cumberland County Naturalizations Index, 1787–1906, Portland Naturalization Record index, 1855–1911, The Famine Immigrants, 1846–1851, Passenger and Immigration Lists Index, Supplements for 1982–1996, Mayflower Families Index

489 Congress St.
Portland, ME 04101
Tel: 207-774-1822

Maine Historical Society:
http://www.mainehistory.org/library_holdings.shtml#immigration

Family Search has the **Maine County Naturalization Records, 1800-1990** index which can be searched for free online

Maine County Naturalization Records, 1800-1990:
https://familysearch.org/search/collection/2040046

Maine Native American Records

Access Genealogy – Maine Native American census records, tribal histories, and much more

Access Genealogy link to:
http://www.accessgenealogy.com/native/maine-indian-tribes.htm

U.S. National Archives - information on American Indians who maintained their ties to Federally-recognized Tribes (1830-1970).

U.S. National Archives: http://www.archives.gov/research/native-americans/

Records of the Bureau of Indian Affairs (BIA)

Records of the Bureau of Indian Affairs (BIA):
http://www.archives.gov/research/guide-fed-records/groups/075.html

American Indians Records Repository - records dating from the 1700s including trust, education and other historic Indian Affairs records

American Indian Records Repository
Meritex Enterprises
17501 West 98th Street
Lenexa, KS 66219
Phone: 913-888-0601

American Indians Records Repository:
http://www.doi.gov/ost/records_mgmt/american-indian-records-repository.cfm

Missing Matriarchs – Resources for Researching Female Maine Ancestors

Looking for female ancestors requires an adjustment of how we view traditional records sources. A woman's identity was often under that of her husband, and often individual records for them can be difficult to locate. The following resources are effective in locating female ancestors in Maine where traditional records may not reveal them.

<u>Bibliographies</u>

1. *Women of Maine,* Lee Agger (Ganner Books, 1982)
2. *Massachusetts and Maine Families,* Walter Goodwin Davis (Genealogical Publishing Co., 1996)
3. *Maine Families in 1790, 5 Vols.* Ruth Gray (Picton Press, 1988-96)
4. *Name Index to Maine Local Histories,* Marie Estes (Maine Historical Society, 1985)
5. *Pioneers of Maine and New Hampshire,* Charles Henry pope Genealogical Publishing Co., 1996)

Selected Resources for Maine Women's History

University of Maine, Farmington Library
111 South Street
Farmington, Maine 04938

Maine Historical Society
489 Congress St.
Portland, ME 04101
Tel: 207-774-1822

Common Maine Surnames

The following surnames are among the most common in Maine and are also being currently researched by other genealogists. If you find your surname here, there is a chance that some research has already been performed on your ancestor.

Abbott, Agnes, Alice, Allen, Amicia, Amsdan, Anarawd, Andersdatter, Andersen, Anderson, Ann, Arthien, Atherton, Ayers, Babbidge, Babson, Baker, Banks, Barents, Barker, Barlow, Barney, Barton, Battisford, Baven, Beeler, Bell, Berry, Best, Bickham, Blaisdell, Blake, Bleddig, Bleddyn, Blodgett, Blood, Bourchier, Boyle, Braci, Brackett, Brett, Bridges, Briggs, Brooks, Brownell, Buxton, Buzzell, Cadell, Cadwr, Cantilupe, Caradog, Castle, Charleton, Cheney, Chesley, Christian, Church, Cillin, Clark, Clarke, Clifford, Clough, Cobb, Coggan, Collier, Cooper, Corbet, Cox, Cram, Crane, Creel, Crocker, Cromwell, Cross, Crossman, Cudworth, Cushman, Cuthbert, Cynan, Cynfyn, Dacre, Daley, Dawson, Day, De Arundel, De Berkeley, De Blancminster, De Blois, De Booley, De Bourgogne, De Bournonville, De Cantilupe, De Cheney, De Clifford, De Cundy, De Dammartin, De Dreaux, De Ewyas, De Fiennes, De Furnes, De Hainault, De Lorraine, De Mons, De Plais, De Plaiz, De Sackville, De Sudeley, De Tingry, De Toni, De Tregoz, Delano, Deschaine, Dorothy, Doughty, Douglas, Dowman, Drane, Drew, Duncanson, Dyfnwallon, Earle, Ednywain, Edwin, Einion, Einudd, Elizabeth, Ellen, Erdington, Estabrook, Farnsworth, Fernald, Fienes, Fiennes, Fillol, Fisher, Fitzhugh, Forrest, Foule, Fowler, Francis, Frank, Fraser, Fremingham, Fruzia, Furbush, Gainfroi, Gardner, Gerberga, Gerrish, Geune, Giddings, Giffard, Giselbert, Goddard, Goodaye, Goold, Gorton, Gould, Gournai, Grant, Griffin, Gronwy, Gruffudd, Gruffyd, Gwaethfoed, Gwair, Gwaithfoed, Gwerystan, Gwrydr, Gwyn, Gwynnian, Hall, Ham, Hampden, Hannah, Hanson, Hapgood, Harper, Hartford, Hartridge, Harwood, Haskell, Hassey, Hawise, Hawsie, Hayden, Hayes, Hayward, Head, Hefferland, Hicks, Hill, Hiller, Hilton, Hobbs, Holland, Holmes, Hopton, Howe, Howland, Hubbard, Hunstanton(Brun), Huntress, Hussey, Hutchins, Hymeid, Hywel,

Iago, Idwal, Ingersoll, Iorworth, James, Joan, Joanna, Johnson, Jones, Jordan, Judd, Judith, Katherine, Keefe, Kelley, Kelsey, Ketchum, Keylynge, Kiinicut, Killoway, Knight, Kumiscza, Kumiszcza, Lagbolt, Lambert, Lamberts, Lane, Lapham, Lawrence, Lawton, Le Brun, Le Strange, Legard, Leighton, Lincoln, Littlefield, Lles, Llewelyn, Lluddica, Llywarch, Llywelyn, Lobdell, Lord, Loring, Lott, Lumpkin, Madistard, Madog, Mallory, Manier, Maplet, Maredydd, Margaret, Margerie, Margery, Martha, Martin, Mary, Matravers, Mavisyn, Maxfield, Mayberry, Maynard, McCann, McConnell, Meacham, Meader, Meads, Merfyn, Merrick, Merrill, Merrow, Messenger, Meurig, Millett, Mistress, Moore, Morse, Morton, Mott, Mowry, Murray, Mynchen, Nash, Naylor, Neal, Neiniad, Nevens, Neville, Nicholson, Nute, Nutter, O'Brien, O'Olaf, Osgood, Owain, Palmer, Parker, Perriman, Petersen, Petronilla, Phippen, Pill, Plumb, Potter, Powers, Poyner, Pratt, Pray, Preble, Quinn, Rebecca, Regnier, Rhodri, Richardson, Ricker, Ricketson, Roberts, Robinson, Rockwood, Rogers, Ross, Rowlandson, Rundall, Russell, Sackville, Sampson, Sanders, Sarah, Saunders, Sawyer, Say, Scullard, Seisyll, Shattuck, Shaw, Shaybery, Shepherd, Sheren, Sherman, Silsby, Simonds, Slocum, Small, Smith, Smythe, Somes, Soule, Sprague, Sproul, Standish, Staples, Starks, Starkweather, Stone, Streeter, Sturry, Susan, Sutton, Sweetman, Sybil, Tallman, Taylor, Thickiness, Thomas, Thomsen, Thurston, Thurstune, Tibbets, Titcomb, Tobey, Towle, Trahaearn, Treadway, Tripp, Trynor, Tucker, Tudur, Tybbot, Unknown, Valiance, Van Loring, Verch, Von Dagsburg, Wallis, Walworth, Ward, Warner, Waste, Waters, Weeks, Wells, Wetherbee, Wheatleigh, Wheatley, Wheeler, Wheelock, Whitcomb, White, Whitney, Wilbore, Wilcox, Wilder, Wilton, Wing, Winslow, Witham, Witherby, Wood

About the Author

Gary L. Morris worked from 2009 to 2014 as a professional researcher for a major player in the genealogy field. After tracing his family lineage back to 1683, he found that genealogy could be an expensive undertaking. As such, has decided to publish these helpful guides to share the valuable free information he has discovered during his career to help others trace their family lineages as inexpensively as possible. An avid genealogist himself, he hopes you will find this guide factual, thorough, helpful, and most of all, effective in helping you to find your family members.

Notes

Notes